The Germans

Greg Nickles

CRABTREE
Publishing Company
www.crabtreebooks.com

CRABTREE
Publishing Company
www.crabtreebooks.com

PMB 16A, 350 Fifth Avenue
Suite 3308
New York, NY 10118

612 Welland Avenue
St. Catharines, Ontario
L2M 5V6

Co-ordinating editor: Ellen Rodger
Content editor: Kate Calder
Production co-ordinator: Rosie Gowsell
Assistant editor: Lisa Gurusinghe

Prepress: Embassy Graphics

Printer: Worzalla Publishing Company

Created by:
Brown Partworks Ltd
Commissioning editor: Anne O'Daly
Project editor: Clare Oliver
Picture researcher: Adrian Bentley
Designer: Abdul Rafique
Maps: Mark Walker
Consultant: Professor Donald Avery, Ph.D. History

CATALOGING-IN-PUBLICATION DATA
Nickles, Greg, 1969-
    The Germans / Greg Nickles
    p.cm. – (We came to North America)
    Includes index.
    ISBN 0-7787-0191-3 (RLB) – ISBN 0-7787-0205-7 (pbk.)
    1. German Americans–History–Juvenile literature. 2. German Americans–Biography–Juvenile literature. 3. United States–Civilization–German influences–Juvenile literature [1. German Americans–History]   I. Title. II. Series.
    E184.G3 N49 2001
    973'.0431–dc21
            00-069356
            LC

Photographs
AKG London 16 (bottom). Brown Partworks Library of Congress 17 (top); National Archives 21. Corbis 16 (top); Adam Woolfitt 24; Angelo Hornak 31 (top); Bettmann 23, 30; Nik Wheeler 25 (bottom). Glenbow Archives, Calgary, Canada (NA-2676-4) 4; (NC-6-851) 11 (bottom); (NA-264-1) 14; (NA-1752-14) 20 (top). Hulton Getty title page, 11 (top), 15 (bottom), 22 (top). Hutchison Library John Wright 20 (bottom). Image Bank Archive Photos 5 (top). K-W Oktoberfest Inc. 28 (bottom). Kobal Collection 22 (bottom). Jason Lavré (cover) North Wind Picture Archives 7, 9 (top), 9 (bottom), 10 (top), 13, 15 (top), 19. Peter Newark's Pictures 5 (bottom), 6, 8, 10 (bottom), 17 (bottom), 25 (top), 27, 28 (top), 29, 31 (bottom).

Special thanks to Waldemar Butz and the Butz family for the family photo that appears on the title page.

Cover: A German bandmember proudly wears lederhosen during a parade.

Book Credits
pages 12, 18, and 26: Library of Congress, Manuscript Division, WPA Federal Writers' Project Collection.

Contents

Introduction

German **immigrants** and their **descendants** have lived in North America for more than 400 years. The first Germans in North America sailed and landed with some of the earliest European explorers in the 1500s. In the early 1600s, a few German tradespeople moved to the settlement of Jamestown in the British **colony** of Virginia. German immigrants soon began arriving in a steady stream throughout the 1600s and 1700s. They settled first in the British colonies along the east coast of what is now the United States. In the last half of the 1800s, German immigration reached its peak and then continued on a smaller scale throughout the 1900s.

The Germans did not come only from lands that were part of Germany. Many came from German-speaking communities in the countries that surround Germany, including Austria, Poland, Switzerland, and Russia. Germans from each land brought their own distinct customs to their new homes in North America.

▼ Andreas Lilge and his family *emigrated* from Russia in 1893. They were among the first German settlers at Bruderheimer, Alberta.

4

Germans came to North America for many reasons. Some came to practice their religion without fear of the punishment they suffered in their homeland. Others came fleeing wars, **famine**, or poverty in Europe. Many came to find new work and share in the wealth of the New World.

Today, millions of German immigrants and their descendants have made important contributions to both the United States and Canada. German tradespeople provided early settlements with the skilled labor needed to build industries. Since then, German immigrants and their descendants have done well in the arts, science, literature, journalism, politics, industry, and sports.

German influences can be seen in the hundreds of North American cities and towns named after German settlements in Europe. Some of these include Bismarck in North Dakota, Anaheim in California, New Braunfels in Texas, Bruderheimer in Alberta, and Berlin, now called Kitchener, in Ontario.

▲ Many German customs, such as giving decorated eggs at Easter, have been adopted across North America.

Judaism and Christianity

Most German immigrants belonged to one of two religions, **Christianity** or **Judaism**. Judaism is an ancient religion based upon the teachings of a holy book called the Torah. The vast majority of German immigrants were Christians, who followed the teachings of Jesus Christ. A few belonged to the **Roman Catholic** Church, but most were **Protestants**, whose church had split away from the Roman Catholic Church during the 1500s. Followers of both kinds of Church had waged war on one another in Germany and across Europe. In the 1930s, many Jews, or followers of Judaism, moved to North America after the **Nazi** government had taken control of Germany. The Nazis hated non-Christians and **persecuted** many Jews.

▲ A Nazi poster from the 1930s depicts Jews as evil and dirty. It is an example of the *anti-Semitism*, toward Jews that was common before and during World War II.

A Proud Heritage

The country of Germany formed in 1871, but the German people trace their **origins** back thousands of years. Their **ancestors**, who lived in many groups, first settled throughout Central Europe around 100 B.C. In ancient times, they were known as strong warriors, who fought and defeated the **Romans** many times.

The German people who lived in Central Europe thousands of years ago belonged to Germanic tribes also known as **Teutonic** tribes. In 9 A.D., a Germanic tribe defeated the Romans in a battle. The defeat stopped the Roman Empire from expanding west of the Rhine river. For hundreds of years, the tribes prospered and became small Germanic kingdoms.

By 500 A.D., the Roman Empire had completely collapsed. Central Europe became a patchwork of hundreds of German kingdoms. German language and **culture** thrived and the Roman Catholic Church **converted** people to Christianity. The German kingdoms often went to war with each other over land, religion, and control of trade. A kingdom called the Franks conquered most of the other kingdoms.

▲ Wilhelm I, the King of Prussia, became the first emperor of a united Germany in January 1871. The ceremony was held at the Palace of Versailles, France.

The "Forty-Eighters"

In 1848, in German lands and throughout Europe, people took up arms against their kings. They fought to set up **democratic** governments, in which leaders are elected by the people, instead of just inheriting the job. When the German rebels lost their battle for democracy, about 10,000 decided to move to the United States, where the government was already democratic. They were known as Forty-Eighters. Unlike most other German immigrants who were farmers or tradespeople who were caught up in the struggle of their homeland, many Forty-Eighters were outstanding **scholars** and **political activists**. They became leaders in politics, journalism, and the arts. They used their influence to help their local German-American communities. They also fought for causes such as freedom for slaves, voting rights, free schools, and labor unions.

▲ The 1848 uprising in Berlin was defeated, and the people failed to found a democratic Germany.

In the early 1800s, 39 German states formed an alliance with the Hapsburg **Empire**, which was based in Austria. The state of Prussia became powerful under the politician, Otto von Bismarck. He was mainly responsible for founding modern Germany, which was made up of Prussia and other states. The remaining kingdoms with German-speaking people became part of the neighboring countries.

The history of Germany up to the early 1900s is marked by historic achievements, scientific discoveries, and the building of great palaces and cathedrals. Life for ordinary Germans was not comfortable. Wars and famines devastated their lands. Germans looked to the colonies in North America as places to escape.

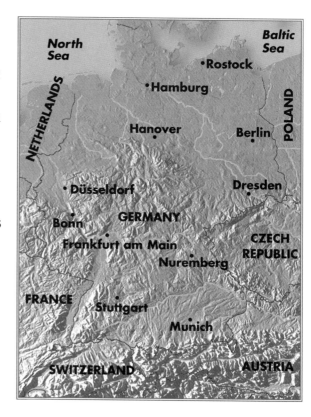

▶ A map of Germany as it is today.

Germantown

In 1683, a group of immigrants founded the first German community in North America, which became known as Germantown. They wanted to escape the unfair treatment they suffered at the hands of other Christians in Europe.

Tired of the unfair ways in which many Protestants were treated, William Penn of England dreamed of making a **refuge** where people were free to worship as they wished. Penn was a member of the Quakers, or Society of Friends, a group of Protestants that believed strongly in peace, equality, and community. In 1681, the British king gave Penn land in North America to set up a new colony, named Pennsylvania. Protestant settlers from Europe were invited to his refuge.

In 1683, thirteen Quaker families from the town of Krefield, in western Germany, accepted Penn's invitation and sailed in the *Concord*, to Philadelphia, Pennsylvania. There, they were joined by another German, Franz Daniel Pastorius, a lawyer who became their leader. Pastorius helped the families obtain land, six miles (ten kilometers) northwest of Philadelphia.

It took a lot of hard work to set up the new community called Germantown. The settlers had only enough time to dig and cover the cellars of their homes before cold weather set in. They spent their first winter underground. Once spring came, they continued building their log homes and clearing trees to make fields for their crops.

Part of Germantown's success lay in the town's design, which helped encourage the settlers to form a strong community. Instead of building large scattered farms, the German homes were built close together to form a small town, complete with vegetable and flower gardens. Larger crops were grown in surrounding fields outside the town.

▲ Settlers gather for a Quaker meeting in Pennsylvania. At such meetings, Quakers worshiped and made decisions about how the community was run.

The Reformation

In the early 1500s, a German priest, Martin Luther, challenged the authority of the Roman Catholic Church. Luther, like many others, believed the leaders of the Church had grown **corrupt**. He believed that only God, not religious leaders, had the power to forgive people's sins. Soon, Luther and other protesters, called Protestants, broke away from the Roman Catholic Church to form their own churches. This split, called the Reformation, led Roman Catholics and Protestants into arguments, violence, and wars. The Protestants formed many different **sects** and some disagreed with others over how to worship. Religious struggles broke out between Protestant sects. Throughout Europe, people from Protestant groups, such as the Quakers, experienced **prejudice** from other Protestants who outnumbered them.

◄ Martin Luther's criticism of the Church changed Christianity forever. The Lutheran Church is a Protestant sect named after him.

▼ William Penn made peace treaties with the Native Americans who lived in Pennsylvania.

The inhabitants of Germantown were finally free to worship without fear of punishment. They could now focus on work. In addition to farming to supply their own needs, they were skillful weavers of linen. Germantown soon **prospered** by selling materials to companies in Philadelphia. By the mid-1700s, Germantown's success encouraged other German Protestants to move there. Germantown's industries expanded to include tanning leather, printing, woodworking, and papermaking.

Germantown became more than a thriving community. Its success proved to other settlers that German immigrants were valuable additions to their communities. It provided an example for other new settlements, and raised hope among Germans in Europe that they could lead successful lives in North America.

The Search for Religious Freedom

Prejudice and violence between Christians in Europe continued throughout the late 1600s and the 1700s.

More German immigrants arrived in the British colonies. Although there was also prejudice and violence in North America, many Protestants enjoyed more freedom of worship there, than in Europe.

Germans from small Protestant sects were especially attracted to Pennsylvania. These sects included Quakers, Amish, Moravians, Mennonites, Dunkers, and Hutterites. They settled in farming areas in Pennsylvania, in counties such as Lehigh, Berks, Lebanon, Lancaster, and York. These sects often held beliefs that were different from those of other Protestants. For example, they shared all money and property, dressed in plain clothing, and did not have **clergy**. Work, family time, and friendships all centered around worship. Their communities often avoided contact with the rest of society.

▲ The Dunkers held gatherings called "love feasts," where the whole community joined together to eat.

◄ German Moravians at prayer. The Moravians founded settlements at Salem in North Carolina, and Nazareth, Lititz, and Bethlehem in Pennsylvania.

Pennsylvania Dutch Today

Today, the term Pennsylvania Dutch is used to describe the population of Old Order Mennonite and Amish people of Pennsylvania. Being Old Order, means that they imitate the way their ancestors lived and isolate themselves from the rest of society to maintain their religious beliefs. Many work as farmers or tradespeople. Most of the Old Order communities still speak mostly German. They wear plain clothes because they believe people should not feel more important than others based on the clothing they wear. They choose to live a simple life without electricity, indoor plumbing, automobiles, and other machinery. Many Amish use modern devices and appliances, such as calculators, refrigerators, and gas stoves. In the 1880s, many Mennonite families moved to Canada. Today, there is a large Old Order Mennonite community in Waterloo, Ontario and other smaller ones on the prairies.

▲ **An Amish family rides to town in an open buggy. They are allowed to ride in cars, but choose not to own cars. They believe in having a simple lifestyle.**

▼ **St. John's First German Lutheran Church, founded in Edmonton, Alberta.**

Together, these groups were called the "Pennsylvania Dutch." The English speakers who lived nearby had confused the word "Dutch" with the name the settlers used for themselves, *Deutsch*, which means German.

Most German immigrants belonged to the Lutheran and Reformed Churches. They were Protestant, but did not have as many strict rules. Lutheran and Reformed Germans settled in New York, Pennsylvania, Virginia, Georgia, the Carolinas, and in Ontario, and Nova Scotia in Canada. In the 1700s, about 100,000 Germans immigrated to North America.

In the 1800s, Germans continued to come in search of religious freedom. Thousands of Lutherans, Mennonites, and Hutterites came from Russia. Their ancestors had moved there in the late 1700s to escape war and prejudice, but, by the late 1800s, Russia was no longer safe. By the 1920s, about 100,000 of these Volga, or Black Sea, Germans, named after the areas of Russia they came from, had moved to the United States and Canada.

Eyewitness to History

MAX RICHTER was born in 1864 in Saxony, a region of northwest Germany. He trained as a cabinetmaker, but life was hard in Germany, even for those people who knew a trade. At the age of seventeen, Richter emigrated, in the hope of making a better life for himself.

"

Most of the people were farmers where we lived in the Saxony part of Germany. The highest wage paid for a farmhand was three dollars a week, and living expenses had to come out of this. To **cure** fine wood such as black walnut took from two to three years, therefore we had to be very saving with our wood. The prospect for getting ahead being very small, and, then, every male had to serve a time out in the army, I decided in the year 1881 to try my fortune in the new country many of my countrymen were coming to — America. So I embarked on the passenger boat, the *Ethiopia*, and, in nineteen days, I landed in New York. From there, I went by boat to Galveston, Texas, then moved to Austin County.

But there were very few of my nationality at this place, and we were anxious for our comrades from the old country. So we then moved to Gillespie County, Texas, and lived near the town of Fredericksburg. This was mostly a German settlement. We kept up our way of getting together which we had in Germany…only we were not as free in Germany as in America. Truly, we found this new country of America to be the "land of the free."

"

The Journey

The journeys that Germans took to get to North America in the 1600s, 1700s, and 1800s were long, difficult, and often filled with danger. Many people fled their homelands in fear of violence or famine.

In Germany, as in other lands, the emigrants left behind family and friends, most of whom they never saw again. Even getting to the ships was difficult. Some took boats to reach departure points, while others went on foot. Twenty-thousand German Lutherans were forced out of Salzburg, Austria, in 1731. Many froze to death on the road to a port.

Sailing ships brought German immigrants to North America's east coast. Most ships were designed to carry cargo, not people, which made the journey very uncomfortable. The voyage took months and many passengers, especially those weakened by famine, died of diseases such as typhus and cholera. Violent storms also claimed countless lives. In the mid-1800s, steamships were introduced. On a steamship, the journey took a matter of weeks, and fewer people died of disease at sea.

▲ **A steamboat carrying Mennonite immigrants arrives at Winnipeg, Manitoba, in 1874.**

◄ **The first German immigrants moved to the British colonies along the east coast. Skilled tradespeople moved inland to booming cities, such as Pittsburgh, Cincinnati, and Chicago. Eventually, the area between Cincinnati, Milwaukee, and St. Louis became known as the "German Triangle," as more and more German immigrants settled there.**

Redemptioners

In the 1600s and 1700s, more than half of the German immigrants to North America could not afford to pay for their voyage across the Atlantic. Instead of staying in Europe, they became redemptioners. Redemptioners agreed to work from four to seven years — or even longer — for anyone who paid for their trip once they arrived. Some immigrants were met by family members or friends already living in America who redeemed, or payed for them. Many had no family waiting and were redeemed by strangers. As a result, families were often split up and forced to work their term apart.

In the early years, colonies were happy to receive immigrants. Passengers **disembarked** with little paperwork or inspection. This all changed in the 1800s. Those who could not work were often turned away and the sick were **quarantined** on their ship or in a hospital.

New York City's Ellis Island became the port of entry for millions of Germans and other immigrants. Upon arrival, wealthy passengers, who traveled in first class, were immediately allowed to enter the country. Most German immigrants could only afford to travel in second class or steerage, which were the cheapest areas. Even if they were healthy enough to be allowed to disembark, they still had to pass many tests before they were able to leave Ellis Island.

▲ The first stage of the long and difficult trip to North America was reaching the busy port of Hamburg, in northern Germany.

◄ This family of Russian Germans arrived at Ellis Island on the *SS Pretoria*. The paper pinned to the father's jacket shows the family has passed inspection.

Settling in North America

Over the centuries, German immigrants settled across the continent. They either founded new farms and communities or moved into German neighborhoods in existing towns and cities.

German tradespeople, such as clockmakers, carpenters, weavers, and glassblowers, settled in towns where their skills were needed. Farmers headed to the countryside.

Once the immigrants settled in, they found ways to feel more at home. They built their own churches, which served as meeting places for their communities. They also established new schools. One of the earliest German schools was Concordia College in Fort Wayne, Indiana, founded in 1840.

In the 1700s, German immigrants began to set up charities, such as Philadelphia's German Society for the Protection of Immigrants, to help newcomers find work, shelter, and friends. At the same time, German workers' groups encouraged laborers to fight for better wages and working conditions.

▲ Germantown's bicycle club was a good opportunity for young and old alike to socialize and stay fit.

◀ Farmers moved to the countryside. They cut down trees to clear land for their crops. The timber was used to build their new homes.

Another way in which Germans made a difference in their new communities was in their local governments and the military. Many Germans became mayors, governors, or other high-ranking officials. One of the most famous German politicians was Jacob Leisler, who became governor of New York in 1689. At the time, New York was a British colony. A militia officer, Leisler became a hero for giving colonists a voice in government. He was executed by the British for his actions in 1691.

By the 1900s, German descendants had made it all the way into the White House. U.S. Presidents Herbert Hoover, elected in 1928, and Dwight D. Eisenhower, elected in 1952, were both of German ancestry.

While religion, work, school, and politics were important to their lives, Germans also got together for fun. German brass bands and singing societies were set up in many cities. Social clubs were founded for theater, and sports such as gymnastics and cycling, along with lodges, or meeting houses, for the Freemasons, an all-male charitable organization.

▲ Some theaters put on shows in German. These performances were a chance for the whole community to come together.

Westward Bound

Many Germans were pioneers who settled the western United States and Canada. The Pennsylvania Dutch invented the Conestoga wagon, the most popular form of transportation used on the journey west. A single wagon carried so much cargo that as many as six horses or oxen were needed to pull it.

The Conestoga wagon was named after the valley in Lancaster County, Pennsylvania, where it was first made. The Conestoga Valley itself, was named after the group of Native Americans who lived in the region.

▲ The Conestoga was large and rugged. It was curved up at the front and back to stop its contents from spilling out on bumpy roads.

Eyewitness to History

**ELIZA BRANDES was born in Sage, Germany, in 1858.
When she was eight years old, her parents sold their
farm in Germany and emigrated to the United States.
It was almost a year before her father finally found
suitable land to settle in Nebraska.**

" My father and mother had a log house on their homestead, and
they had to go and live on it for awhile; and I had to stay on
the home place and do all the chores and housework; and I did
not have much time to go to school regularly.

My father had a pair of heavy work oxen, and they did all
the plowing and other hard work; and, later, he bought a team
of horses for $300. The corn we planted with a small hand
planter. We also had a reaper, but we had to bind all the
grain by hand.

I remember my father had a hard time to find milk cows.
He would drive all over the country, and he finally got four
cows. I remember we had one staked out, and she broke loose
and started to run down a hill and broke her neck.

The Indians used to come to our house so many times.
They came mostly from the Omaha tribe. They would
always ask for some things to eat. At one time, a large band of
them camped close to our place for a whole week. They were
camped close to the creek so they would have plenty of water
and could fish, but they didn't bother us so very much. "

German Language

German immigrants brought with them a rich language. Many of their words have now been adopted into English.

▲ A young Hutterite girl in Alberta practices writing in German.

From the 1600s, the use of the German language in North America grew steadily as more and more German immigrants landed from Europe. The popularity of the language reached its peak in the late 1800s, which was also the time of the highest German immigration. Immigrants spoke German with their family, friends, and other German co-workers. They also learned English so they could speak with other North Americans.

During World War I (1914–1918), in which Germany was an enemy of the United States, and Canada, the German language became unpopular in North America. Many North Americans unfairly began to think of German immigrants as enemies. Using the German language was banned in some places, so people of German **heritage** began using English to avoid prejudice. Many families even switched their names from German to English. They changed their last name from "Schmidt" or "Schmied" to "Smith," from "Braun" to "Brown," or from "Schwarz" to "Black."

◄ The names of popular German foods, such as "pretzel," "wiener," "hamburger," "noodle," and "pumpernickel," have become familiar among North Americans.

From German to English

German and English developed long ago from the same European language, called West Germanic, which was spoken in ancient times. Due to their shared roots, many words in German and English — including "winter," "wind," "hand," and "finger" — are exactly the same. In North America, German words, such as these below, were adopted into the English language from the German immigrants' speech.

English	German	English	German
angst	*Angst* ("anxiety")	leitmotif	*Leitmotiv* ("leading motive or theme")
cookbook	*Kochbuch* ("cookbook")	mishmash	*Mischmasch* ("a jumbled mixture")
hold on	*halt an* ("wait a minute")	waltz	*Walzer* ("roll or dance")
iceberg	*Eisberg* ("iceberg")	wunderkind	Wunder Kind ("wonder child")
kaput	*kaputt* ("out of order")	yodel	*Jodeln* ("to yodel")
kitsch	*Kitsch* ("trash")	zigzag	*Zickzack* ("zigzag")

Today, German is spoken exclusively in only a few places in North America, including parts of Pennsylvania, Texas, and Iowa, in the United States and Manitoba and Ontario in Canada. The Mennonites and Amish are among those who still speak German. Followers of these sects have kept their traditional language and have preserved their unique way of life.

Many German immigrants were pioneers of publishing. Some brought printing skills from Germany, which was the birthplace of the printing press in the 1400s. Many German-language newspapers, magazines, and books were produced in the 1700s and 1800s. The first was a newspaper, printed in 1732 in Philadelphia. Philadelphia soon became a center for publishing. The first bible printed in North America was printed there in 1742.

Reading was a favorite pastime for many German immigrants, and, by 1888, the number of German-language magazines and newspapers had increased to about 800. As their descendants adopted English, many of these publications went out of print. Only a handful of these publications were being published by the end of the 1900s. North America's modern publishing industry owes its beginning to the early German printers.

▼ **This illustrated family record of 1833 was found stuck to the back of a German newspaper.**

Fleeing Hitler's Germany

After the 1800s, the next major wave of German immigration to North America began in the 1930s. Germans came to escape the brutal government of Adolf Hitler.

Following its defeat in World War I (1914–1918), Germany was plagued by riots, unemployment, and poverty. Hoping to put an end to these problems, many Germans began supporting the harsh, racist ideas of the Nazi Party led by Adolf Hitler. In 1933, the Nazis became Germany's government.

Hitler and his supporters believed in running the country through force and violence rather than free speech and voting. They built up Germany's armed forces and attacked its neighboring countries, beginning World War II (1939–1945). Germans who opposed the Nazis were fired from their jobs or arrested. The Nazis hated those who did not have Christian or German ancestry. They were especially brutal to Jews and Eastern Europeans. After taking away their money, possessions, and homes, the Nazis turned millions into slaves or murdered them.

Rather than face the cruelty of the Nazis, hundreds of thousands of German-speaking people escaped Europe. Some had time to pack their bags, but most had to sneak away using false identities, leaving behind all that they owned, for fear of being arrested and killed.

▲ This lawyer was forced to march through the streets of Munich, Germany, during the 1930s. His placard says "I am a Jew but I will never again complain about the Nazis."

▶ Marlene Dietrich was already a successful German movie star when she moved to the United States in 1930. She went on to star in films, such as *Blonde Venus* and *Shanghai Express*.

After World War II

After the Nazis' defeat and the end of World War II, Germans lined up by the thousands to immigrate to North America. Some decided to leave Europe because their country and homes lay in ruins. Many wanted to escape the horrors of the war and live in a more peaceful land. Others were forced to leave in search of work. Immigration to the United States and Canada fell after the 1950s, as farms, industries, and homes in Germany were rebuilt, and people once again enjoyed their lives.

Of those who were lucky enough to escape, more than 100,000 immigrated to North America. These immigrants came from many backgrounds, including expert scholars, scientists, writers, and artists.

Of the scientists who escaped, prize-winning physicist Albert Einstein, was especially important. Einstein was opposed to war, but, in 1940, he wrote to President Franklin Roosevelt, warning him of the danger of the Nazis developing an atomic bomb. Roosevelt set up the Manhattan Project to develop atomic weapons. Many German Jewish scientists worked on this project to create the first atomic bombs, which were used by the United States toward the end of World War II.

North American artists enjoyed the inspiration of German authors, including Thomas Mann and Erich Remarque, who continued their writing careers in the United States. Composers such as Kurt Weill and Arnold Schoenberg and theater director, Max Reinhardt had successful careers in America. The Hollywood film industry also gained talents such as the glamorous actor, Marlene Dietrich.

Not all Germans in North America were well treated. In World War II, many people of German heritage were denied the freedom to travel or work where they wanted because other North Americans feared they might become spies for Germany.

▶ **Albert Einstein was awarded the Nobel Prize for Physics in 1921. Fleeing the Nazis, he immigrated to the United States in 1933.**

German Music and Food

The culture brought over by the millions of German immigrants to North America, over the last 300 years, has had a strong influence on life in the United States and Canada. German foods, for example, have become part of the daily North American diet and German music is a part of celebrations and festivals across the continent.

German immigrants have included many musicians and singers, both professional and **amateur**. They cherished the traditional folk music of their homelands. In singing societies and brass bands, people of German heritage got together to play, sing, dance, or just listen. Marching bands parade in costumes traditionally worn by their ancestors in Germany. Today, such groups perform both old and new music, and they even attract many followers from outside the German community.

▼ German band players dress in the costumes traditionally worn in Bavaria, a region in southeast Germany.

Traditional German bands are often called Bavarian bands, after the region in Germany where they originated. They consist of horns, often accompanied by the clarinet and accordion. The Musicians dress in Bavarian costume — white shirts, vests, and dark shorts or skirts — and play slow waltzes and lively polkas. These dances were popular among people of all ages during the 1800s and early 1900s. Today, they are usually danced at celebrations.

One of the greatest influences German immigrants have had on North American life is with their food. Many German foods are found at special festivals and restaurants. They include fried pieces of breaded veal or pork, called *schnitzel*, sausages such as *bratwurst* and *knackwurst*, and *sauerkraut*, which is made of shredded, pickled cabbage.

Foods inspired by German cooking are found in almost any North American home. Hamburgers were introduced in St. Louis, Missouri, around 1900. Their name comes from the "hamburger steak" of ground beef, eaten by people in Hamburg, Germany. Wieners, also called *frankfurters*, are a type of sausage first made in the German city of Frankfurt. Pickles, ketchup, and other German-prepared foods were popularized in North America by Henry John Heinz.

North America's beer industry, too, was transformed by Germans. Most of its largest breweries were founded in the 1800s by German immigrants or their descendants, including Adolph Coors, Frederick Pabst, and Joseph Schlitz. Today, Anheuser-Busch, the brewery begun by Eberhard Anheuser and Adolphus Busch, produces Budweiser, which is one of the world's best-selling brands of beer.

"Now watch him drop that paper!"

The Beer that made Milwaukee Famous

▲ **This advertisement from the 1940s promotes Schlitz, a German-style beer produced in Milwaukee.**

▼ **German sausages are often served with sauerkraut made of shredded and pickled white cabbage.**

Sweet Treats

Chocolate was first mass-produced by German-American Milton Hershey of Pennsylvania. He perfected the first chocolate bar in 1900 and built the world's largest chocolate factory. Henry Heide, another candy maker of German heritage, invented the fruity gumdrops known as jujubes.

Eyewitness to History

Speaking in 1938, New Yorker WILLIAM WOOD remembered the German folk bands that used to play on the street corners of Brooklyn, before World War I.

" They were composed of instrumentalists numbering from six to a dozen men of various ages and artistic ability. Each group had its own **repertoire**, as well as its peculiar uniforms, which lent an air of distinction and color.

The instruments on which they performed were of that **sonorous** type which interpreted so well the folk-tunes of the fatherland. The saxhorn, tuba, trombone, and cornet were much in evidence.

After two or three choice musical selections **deemed** sufficient to arouse the emotional generosity of the audience, one of the bandsmen would mingle with the assembled crowd, hat in hand, to receive the donations of inspired people.

It was **customary** for the **personnel** of these sidewalk bands to proceed after each concert to the nearest saloon. There, the landlord or bartenders usually **dispensed** free beers and, if it were about mealtimes, the musicians would **regale** themselves with **delectable** morsels of pumpernickel and sausage, so dear to the Teutonic **palate**.

Many of the German bands were composed solely of immigrants. Sometimes a whole group made their home in a single apartment, thus reducing to a minimum the cost of living. As has been shown, they received at least a goodly proportion of their food and beverage **gratis**. "

Traditions and Festivals

Over the last 300 years, German immigrants and their descendants have often celebrated the traditions and holidays of their homelands. Many of their customs and festivals were adopted in turn, by other North Americans.

One of the most famous and widespread German traditions is decorating an evergreen tree at Christmas, the Christian holiday that celebrates Jesus Christ's birth. The tree, which stays green all winter, represents Christ's promise of eternal life to his followers. Some people believe that Germans first began this tradition outdoors over a thousand years ago, using fruits, nuts, and lighted candles as decorations. It is thought that later, in the 1500s, Martin Luther was the first to cut down a Christmas tree and bring it indoors. In the German tradition, the tree is decorated on Christmas Eve by the mother of the household. The children do not see it until it is decorated.

▲ The custom of decorating a fir tree at Christmas was first practiced in Germany.

▼ Dancers perform during the annual Oktoberfest in Kitchener, Ontario. The original Oktoberfest is held each year in Munich, Germany.

Germans and Education

German customs have influenced the education of all North American children. Physical education, a subject emphasized in Germany, was encouraged by a German-American club called the Turnvereins in the second half of the 1800s. The club promoted fitness by setting up athletic facilities and organizing gymnastic competitions.

The word "kindergarten" is German for "nursery school." North America's first kindergarten, similar to the ones in Germany, was started by German immigrant Margaretha Meyer Schurz in 1856.

▲ **Baron von Steuben was born in Germany in 1730. He led U.S. troops in the War of Independence and later became a U.S. citizen.**

Some say the Christmas tree tradition was brought to North America in the late 1700s by German soldiers called Hessians. Others believe that the Pennsylvania Dutch introduced the custom. In Canada, the first Christmas tree is said to have been decorated in 1781 by German General Von Reidesel, in Québec. By the late 1800s, the Christmas tree was widely adopted by other North Americans to brighten their homes.

The Easter holiday, which marks Christ's death and **resurrection**, is also celebrated with German influences. The custom of the Easter bunny, who hides colored or chocolate eggs for children on Easter morning was brought to North America by the Germans.

German history, music, and food are the main attractions at many German festivals celebrated each year in the United States and Canada. These include the famous Steuben Parade, which is held each September in New York City. It honors the contributions of German immigrants during the American Revolution. Its namesake, General Wilhelm von Steuben, helped George Washington train his troops.

Many celebrations are modeled after Oktoberfest, a huge beer festival held each October in Germany. The Canadian twin cities of Kitchener–Waterloo, Ontario, hold the largest Oktoberfest outside of Germany. Hundreds of thousands of people enjoy bands, a parade, and food, that celebrate the diversity of the local German community. To honor Kitchener's history of German immigration, the city holds a Citizenship Court, in which new immigrants get their Canadian citizenship.

Here to Stay

Of the millions of Germans who immigrated to the United States and Canada, and their millions of descendants, many stand out for their great achievements.

Some of the most well-known North Americans of German ancestry, have worked in politics. Carl Schurz was a "Forty-Eighter" who served President Lincoln as a general in the American Civil War (1861–1865), before entering the U.S. Senate. Statesman Henry Kissinger was brought to the United States from Germany by his parents in 1938 to escape the Nazi government. Kissinger was Secretary of State to Presidents Nixon and Ford and received the Nobel Peace Prize in 1973. John D. Diefenbaker from Saskatchewan was Canada's first prime minister of German background, a post he held from 1957 to 1963.

Many Germans brought great skill and ingenuity to the fields of business and industry. John Jacob Astor is said to have arrived in 1784 with just $25. He went on to become the richest man in the United States through his trade in furs and real estate. In 1850, German-American Levi Strauss created the first pair of denim jeans for the North American worker. To this day, "Levi's" is one of the best-selling brand of jeans around the world. In the late 1800s, the Studebaker Brothers Manufacturing Company, owned by the five Studebaker brothers, became the world's leading maker of horse-drawn carriages. They entered the automobile industry in 1902, with the introduction of an electric car. The Studebaker company produced cars until the 1960s.

◄ Opera singer Lotte Lehmann moved to the United States in 1938 and became a U.S. citizen. Here, she plays the role of Elizabeth in Wagner's opera, *Tannhäuser*.

The long list of Germans in North America even includes a saint. John Nepomucene Neumann was a Roman Catholic priest who arrived in the United States in 1836. After his death, people claimed that they were healed while visiting his shrine. He was declared a saint in 1977.

One of the most famous children's storytellers and illustrators, Theodore Seuss Geisel, known as Dr. Seuss by millions of children, was of German ancestry. He was born in Springfield, Massachusetts and began his career as an illustrator and humor writer for magazines and newspapers. He is best known for the books and cartoons he created, including *The Cat in the Hat* and *Green Eggs and Ham*. He also created documentary films and won Academy Awards for his animated cartoons.

▲ **German-born architect Mies van der Rohe designed New York's famous Seagram Building.**

Baseball

Baseball, America's national pastime, has produced many stars of German heritage. One of the brightest was Babe Ruth (left). He was born in 1895 in Baltimore, and is famous for his career with the New York Yankees. For almost 40 years, he held the record for the most home runs. He retired as a player in 1935, and, in 1946, was diagnosed with throat cancer. In his honor, April 27, 1947 was declared "Babe Ruth Day." Ruth died on August 16, 1948. Hundreds of thousands of people turned out to pay their last respects to a baseball legend.

Glossary

amateur A person who practices a skill as a hobby, rather than a job.

ancestor A family member from the past, such as a grandparent.

anti-Semitic hostile toward Jews.

Christianity A religion based on the teachings of Jesus Christ and the Bible.

clergy Religious leaders who lead people in prayer at church.

colony Area of land settled or conquered by a distant state and controlled by it.

convert To change from one religion to another.

corrupt Guilty of bad behavior.

culture A group of people's way of life, including their language, beliefs, and art.

cure To age (wood).

customary Usual practices.

deemed Considered.

democratic Where government is appointed by the people.

delectable Delightful.

descendant A family member, such as a child, or grandchild.

disembark To get off a vehicle.

dispense To give out.

emigrate To leave one's country for another country.

empire Group of countries ruled by one supreme authority.

famine A serious lack of food in a country or area.

gratis Free of charge.

heritage The language, beliefs, lifestyles, and art that people receive from previous generations.

immigrant Someone who comes to settle in one country from another.

Judaism The religion of the Jews, who follow the teachings of a holy book called the Torah.

Nazi A person who followed the racist ideas of the German political party led by Adolf Hitler.

origins Beginnings.

palate Sense of taste.

persecuted: Treated poorly.

personnel Staff or members.

political activists People who protest issues related to politics.

prejudice An unfair opinion.

Protestant A Christian who does not follow the teachings of the Roman Catholic Church.

prosper To become successful.

quarantine Being kept away from other people so that infectious diseases do not spread.

refuge A place safe from danger.

regale To entertain.

repertoire A set of songs that a band knows well and performs.

resurrection The rising of Jesus Christ after his death and burial.

Romans The citizens of the ancient or modern city of Rome.

Roman Catholic A Christian who follows the teachings of the Roman Catholic Church.

scholar a highly educated person.

sect Group of people who have the same religious faith.

sonorous Sounding loud and full.

Teutonic German.

Index

1 2 3 4 5 6 7 8 9 0 Printed in the USA 5 4 3 2 1